VOLCANOES

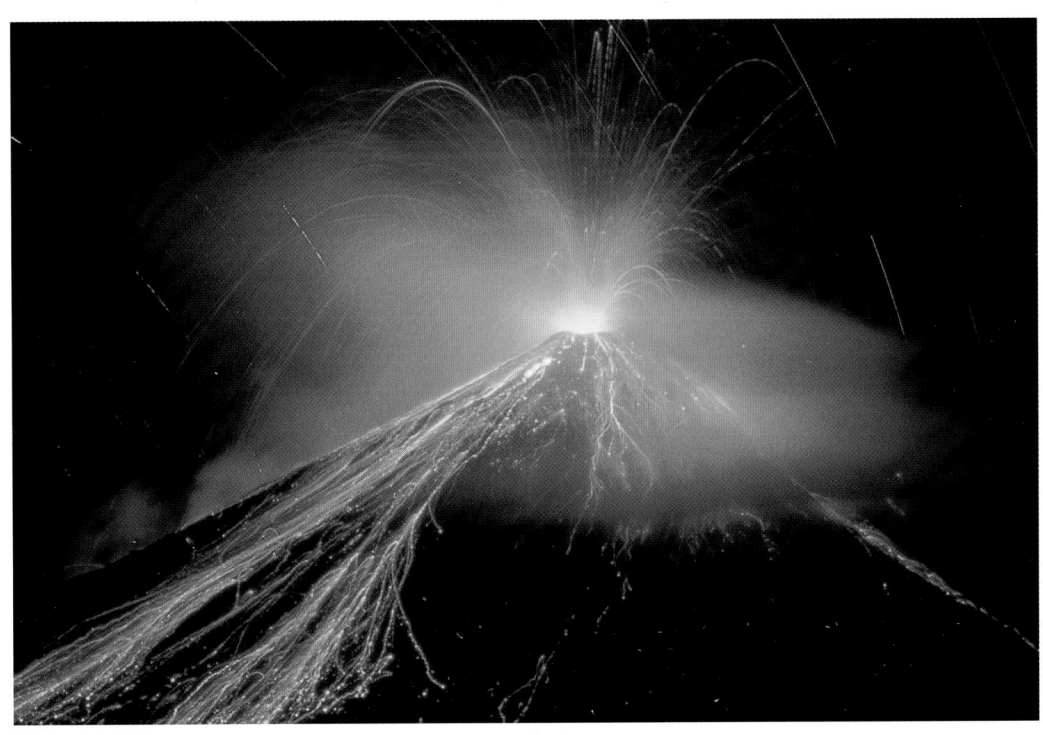

DANIEL ROGERS

HODDER
Wayland

an imprint of Hodder Children's Books

GEOGRAPHY STARTS HERE!

Volcanoes

OTHER TITLES IN THE SERIES
Earthquakes · Hills and Mountains
Maps and Symbols · Rivers and Streams
Weather Around You · Where People Live
Your Environment

Produced for Wayland Publishers Limited by
Roger Coote Publishing
Gissing's Farm
Fressingfield
Suffolk IP21 5SH

Designer: Victoria Webb

Editor: Alex Edmonds

Picture Research: Lynda Lines

Illustrations: Peter Bull

First published in Great Britain in 1998
by Wayland Publishers Ltd

Reprinted in 2002 by Hodder Wayland,
an imprint of Hodder Children's Books

© Hodder Wayland 1998

British Library Cataloguing in Publication Data
Rogers, Daniel, 1955–
Volcanoes. – (Geography starts here!)
1.Volcanoes – Juvenile literature
I.Title
551.2'1

ISBN 07502 4156 X
Printed and bound in Hong Kong

All Wayland books encourage children to read and help them improve their literacy.

- ✓ The contents page, page numbers, headings and index help locate specific pieces of information.

- ✓ The glossary reinforces alphabetic knowledge and extends vocabulary.

- ✓ The further information section suggests other books dealing with the same subject.

Picture Acknowledgements
Pages 1: Image Bank/Richard Ustinich. 5: Bruce Coleman/Werner Stoy.
7: Bruce Coleman/Gerald Cubitt. 8, 9: Photri Inc. 10: Zefa. 12: Getty
Images/Paul Kenward. 13: Bruce Coleman/Orion Service and Trading Co Inc.
15: Bruce Coleman/Fritz Prenzel. 17: Oxford Scientific Films/Breck P
Kent/Earth Scenes. 18: Getty Images/Hideo Kurihara. 19: Photri Inc.
20: Geoscience Features. 21: Rex Features/Pedro Ugarte/Sipa. 22: Rex
Features/Carraro. 23: Photri Inc. 24: Oxford Scientific Films/Richard
Packwood. 25: Geoscience Features/Dr B Booth. 26: Photri Inc.
28: Oxford Scientific Films/Colin Monteath. 29: Rex Features/Yves
Breton/Sipa. 31: Photri Inc. Cover: Zefa.

551.21

The photo on the previous page shows the volcano Arenal in Costa Rica.

CONTENTS

A MOUNTAIN OF FIRE

A volcano is a hole or crack in the surface of the Earth. Out of this hole comes a fiery substance called magma. Magma is made up of rocks that are so hot they have melted.

Magma comes from deep inside the Earth. When it pushes up through a hole and flows on to the surface it is called lava. As the lava cools down it becomes solid rock. Gradually the rock builds up to form a mountain.

This diagram shows the layers of the Earth. We live on the thin, surface layer called the crust.

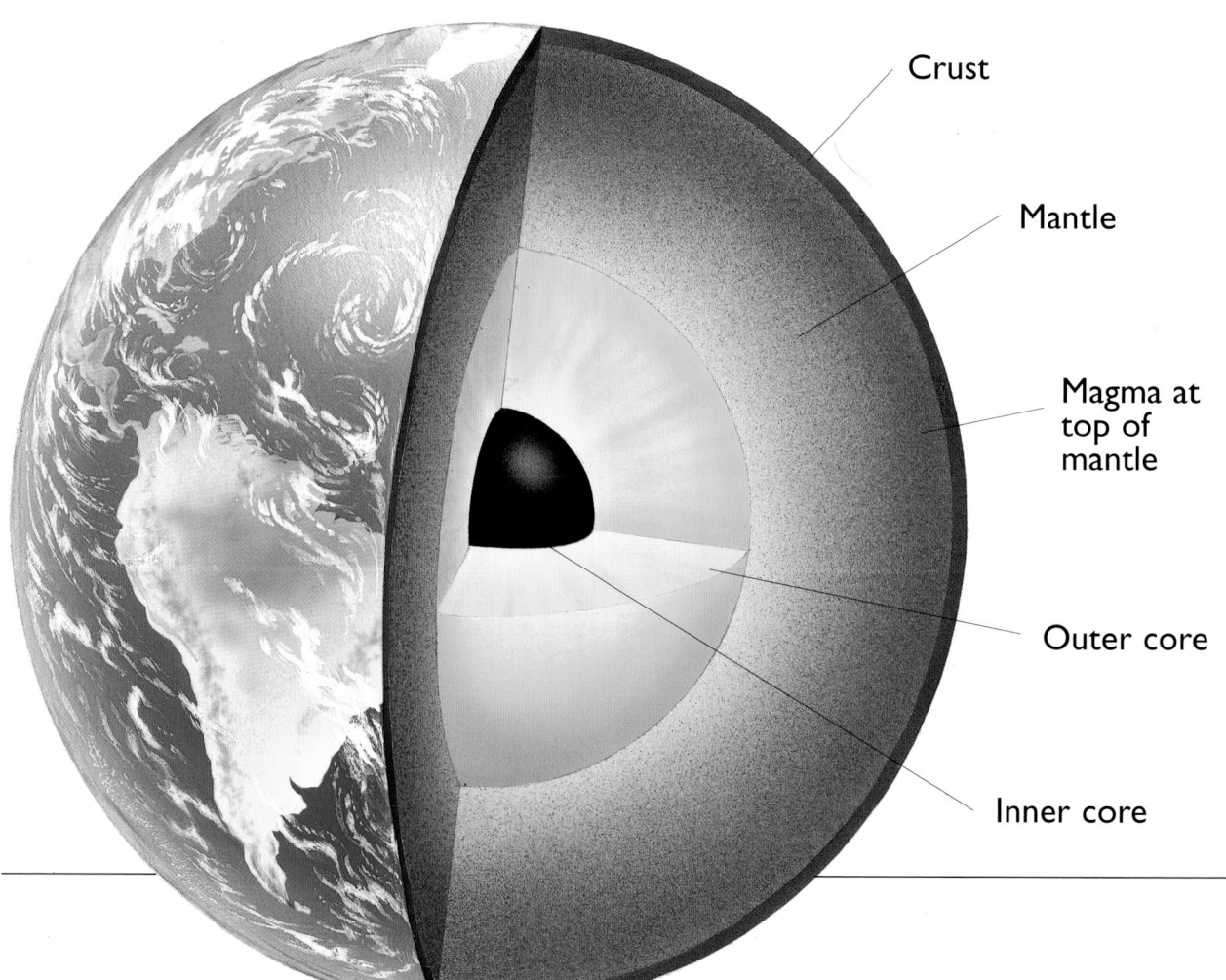

Crust

Mantle

Magma at top of mantle

Outer core

Inner core

Fountains of lava pour out of Kilauea volcano in Hawaii, USA.

THE WORLD'S VOLCANOES

Volcanoes are not found everywhere in the world. Mostly they occur around the edges of the Pacific Ocean, in a huge band called the 'Ring of Fire'.

There are also groups of volcanoes in East Africa, Iceland, southern Italy and the Caribbean. There are even some in the frozen continent of Antarctica.

The Earth's crust is broken into huge pieces called plates. Most volcanoes are near the edges of plates.

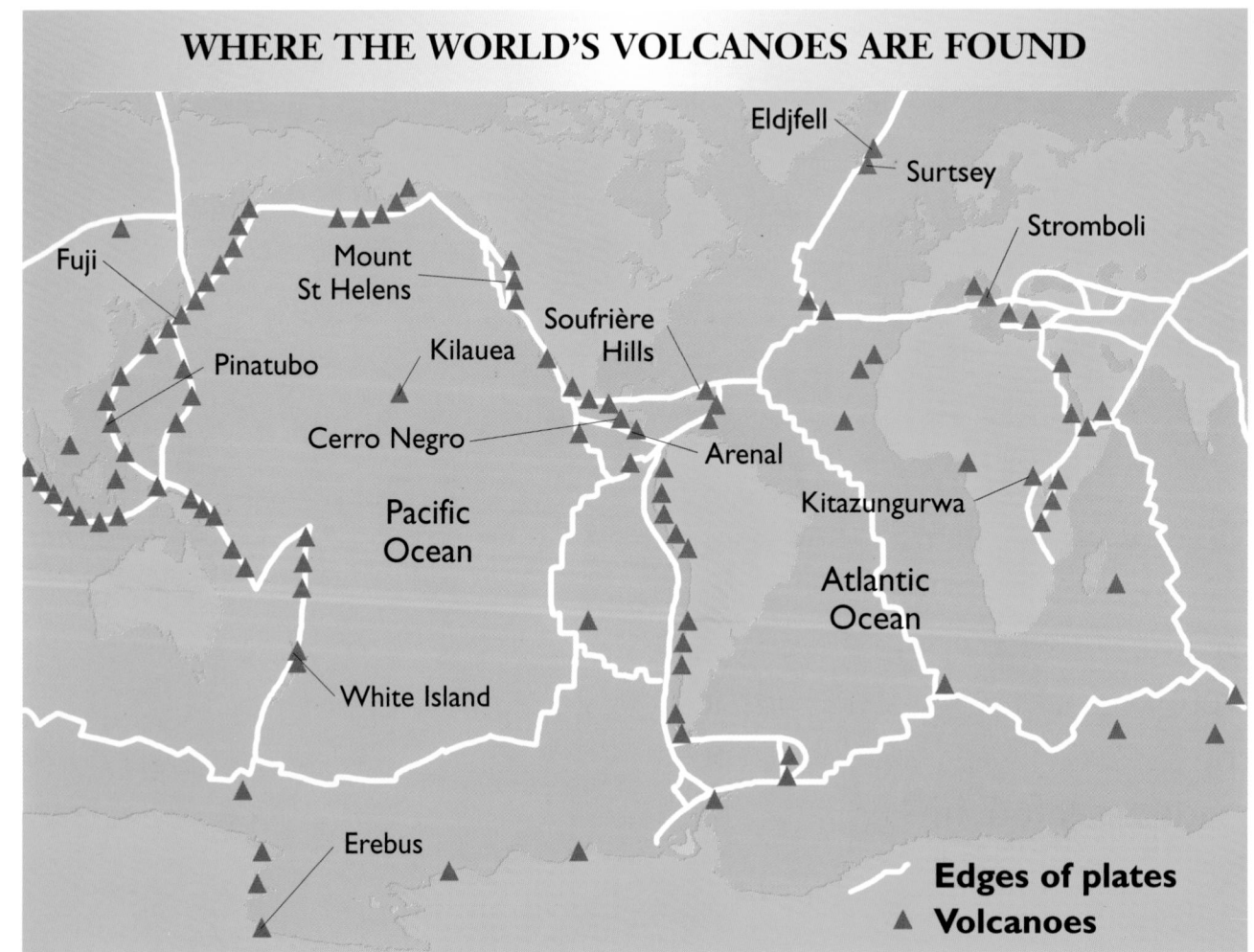

WHERE THE WORLD'S VOLCANOES ARE FOUND

Eldjfell
Surtsey
Stromboli
Fuji
Mount St Helens
Soufrière Hills
Kilauea
Pinatubo
Cerro Negro
Arenal
Kitazungurwa
Pacific Ocean
Atlantic Ocean
White Island
Erebus

Edges of plates
▲ Volcanoes

Once there were volcanoes in many other places, too. Millions of years ago, in parts of Britain, France and North America, there were volcanoes pouring red-hot lava over the land surface. Now, only the rocks they made are left behind.

These volcanoes in Java, Indonesia, are part of the Ring of Fire.

Steam and ash burst from an underwater volcano at the bottom of the Atlantic Ocean.

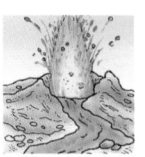

Volcanoes Under the Sea

There are probably more volcanoes under the world's oceans than there are on land. Usually we can't see underwater volcanoes because the oceans are so deep. But sometimes a volcano grows taller and taller until it appears above the surface of the ocean.

The island of Surtsey first appeared off Iceland in 1963. It was made by an underwater volcano.

Some islands in the Atlantic, Pacific and Indian oceans are actually volcanoes.

WHEN A VOLCANO ERUPTS

When magma breaks through the Earth's crust, this is called an eruption. Volcanic eruptions are some of the most powerful forces on Earth. Sometimes a volcano erupts in a huge explosion that can be heard thousands of kilometres away.

When lava pours from a volcano, it may flow towards towns and villages. The people who live there have to run for their lives.

Lava flows like a river from a volcano in Hawaii, USA.

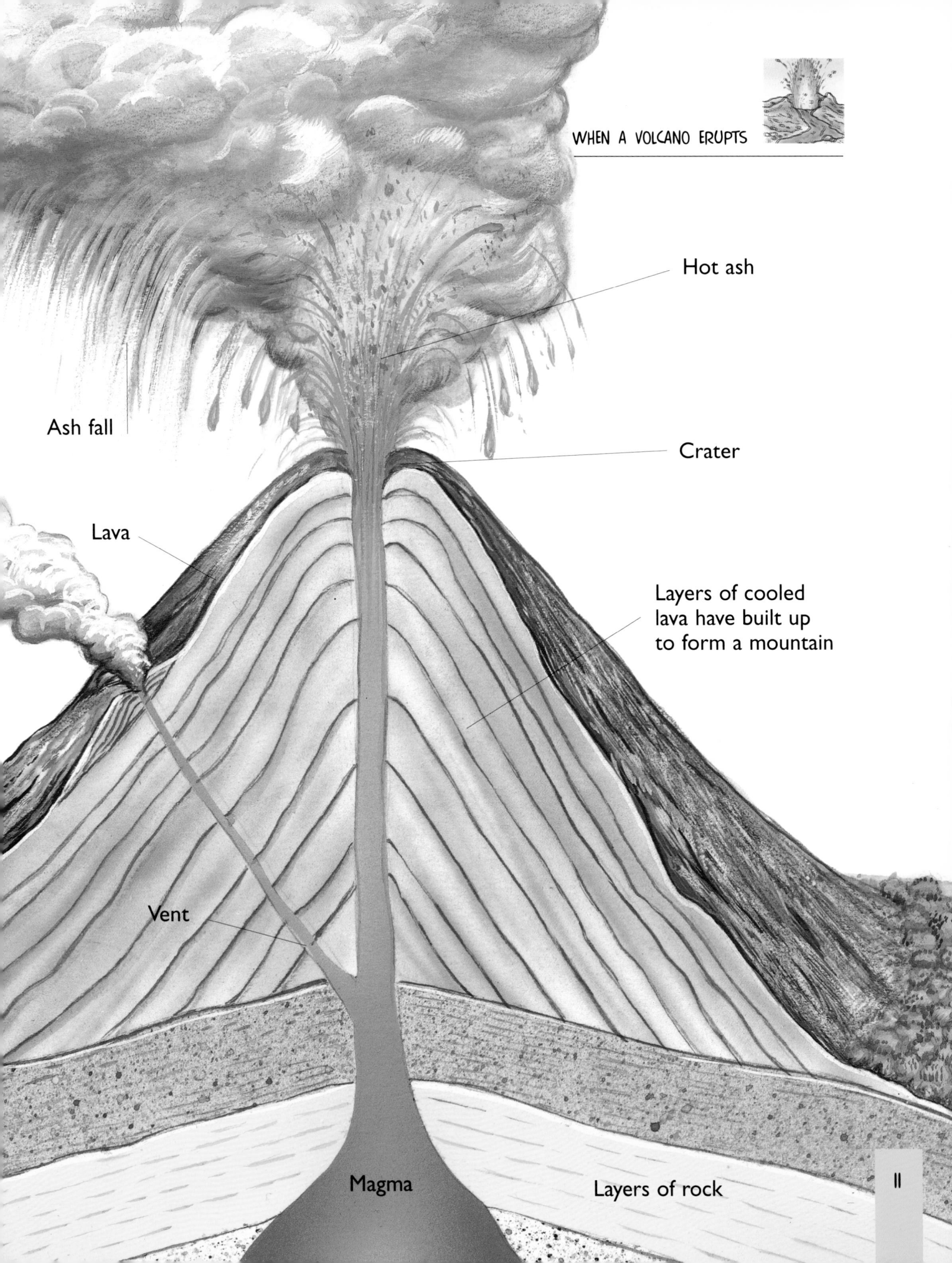

Hot ash

Ash fall

Crater

Lava

Layers of cooled
lava have built up
to form a mountain

Vent

Magma

Layers of rock

Why Volcanoes Erupt

Most volcanoes don't erupt all the time. Although magma is always pushing up towards the surface, it isn't usually strong enough to break through. But eventually the pressure becomes too much, and the magma bursts through weak spots in the crust.

Volcanoes that have not erupted for a long time are called dormant.

White Island volcano in New Zealand is called an active volcano. This means it could erupt at any time.

DISASTER REPORT

Find out as much as you can about the Soufrière Hills volcano that erupted on the Caribbean island of Montserrat in 1997.

Imagine you are a journalist and write a news report describing the eruption. You could draw pictures to illustrate your report.

Fuji, in Japan, is an extinct volcano. This means it has not erupted for hundreds of years.

Volcanic Eruptions

Some eruptions are like explosions. Others are more gentle. If the magma is thin and runny, the gas inside it can escape easily and the magma flows gently from the volcano.

But gas can't escape so easily from thick, sticky magma. As it tries to get out, the pressure builds up until it bursts out and explodes. Bits of magma are blasted into the air.

Strombolian volcano

Ash blown a few kilometres

Explosive eruption

Sticky lava

Hawaiian volcano

Runny lava

Steep sides

Lumps of magma thrown out

Gently sloping sides

Ash falls near volcano

Not all volcanoes erupt in the same way. These diagrams show the main types of eruption.

Stromboli is a volcano in southern Italy. It has given its name to a type of eruption.

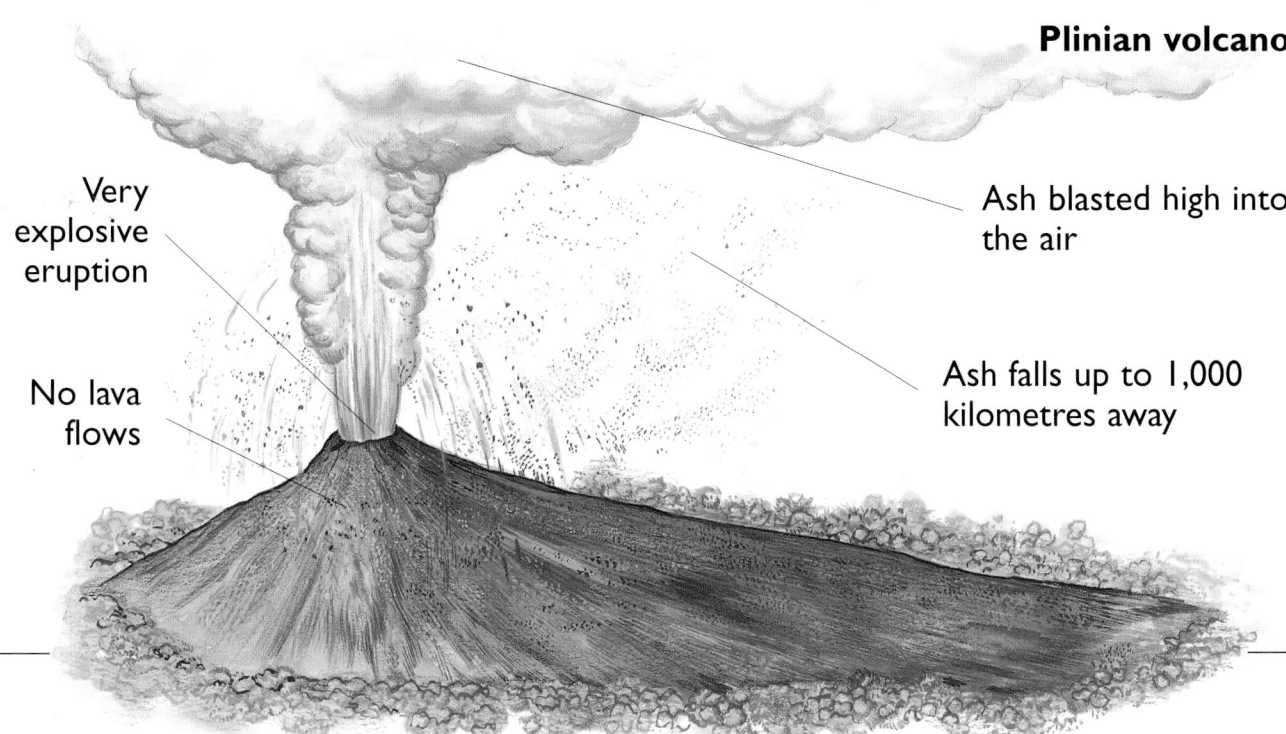

Plinian volcano

Very explosive eruption

No lava flows

Ash blasted high into the air

Ash falls up to 1,000 kilometres away

After an Eruption

When a volcano has erupted, the area around it may suffer very strong winds and heavy rain. The rainwater then mixes with the ash that has poured from the volcano. This mixture becomes a thick mud.

Mud on the sides of the volcano may slide downhill as a mud flow. Mud flows contain thousands of tonnes of mud and travel very fast. They destroy everything in their way.

The town of Armero, Colombia, was buried by a mud flow in 1985.

When Mount St Helens, USA, erupted in 1980, a huge flow of mud, rock and ice destroyed all these trees.

Hot water and steam shoot from a geyser in Rotorua, New Zealand.

Geysers and Mud Pools

In volcanic areas, magma under the ground heats up water that is in the rocks. In some places, the heated water and steam may come to the surface gently in hot springs. In others they may spurt up from the ground as a geyser.

Hot springs sometimes produce large pools of mud at the surface. Hot water and steam bubble up through the mud.

The bubbles of steam make a 'plop' sound as they burst in a mud pool.

PEOPLE AND VOLCANOES

Volcanoes can cause terrible damage. Lava flowing over the ground can cover buildings and crops and set them on fire.

The ash that is blown out of a volcano is even more destructive. Huge amounts of ash may fall to the ground like a heavy, grey snowfall. The ash can be so thick that fields, houses and whole towns are buried under it.

This house is being buried by lava from Eldjfell volcano, Iceland.

Thick clouds of ash pour from Cerro Negro volcano in Nicaragua. The ash makes it difficult for people to breathe.

Rescue workers help survivors after a mud flow in Armero, Colombia.

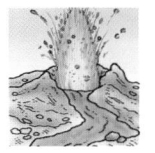

DANGER ZONE

Imagine your home is on the slopes of a volcano. With your friends, act out what you would do if the volcano erupted. If you had to leave your home and you could take only one thing with you, what would you choose?

Fifty-seven people were killed when Mount St Helens erupted in 1980.

Volcanic Killers

Volcanoes can bring death as well as destruction. Most people are killed by falling ash, mud flows and ash flows. An ash flow is a red-hot cloud of volcanic dust that hurtles downhill at over 100 kilometres per hour.

In 1991, Pinatubo in the Philippines erupted. Over 700 people were killed by mud flows, ash flows and by diseases caused by the poisonous ash.

VOLCANOES AND THE ENVIRONMENT

Ash that is blown into the air in an eruption can affect the world's weather for months afterwards. The ash blocks out some of the Sun's rays, making the temperature colder.

Poisonous gases from volcanoes can cause acid rain. When the gases mix with water in the air, they make acid. The acid then falls to the ground as rain. Acid rain can kill trees and poison lakes and rivers.

Ash from Kitazungurwa volcano has killed these trees in Zaire.

Volcanic ash and dust in the air can make beautiful sunsets.

Useful Volcanoes

Volcanoes are not always bad. Soil that is made from volcanic lava contains minerals that help plants to grow. This means the soil is very good for farming. Many crops are grown on the slopes of volcanoes.

Rice is grown in the rich volcanic soil of Bali, Indonesia.

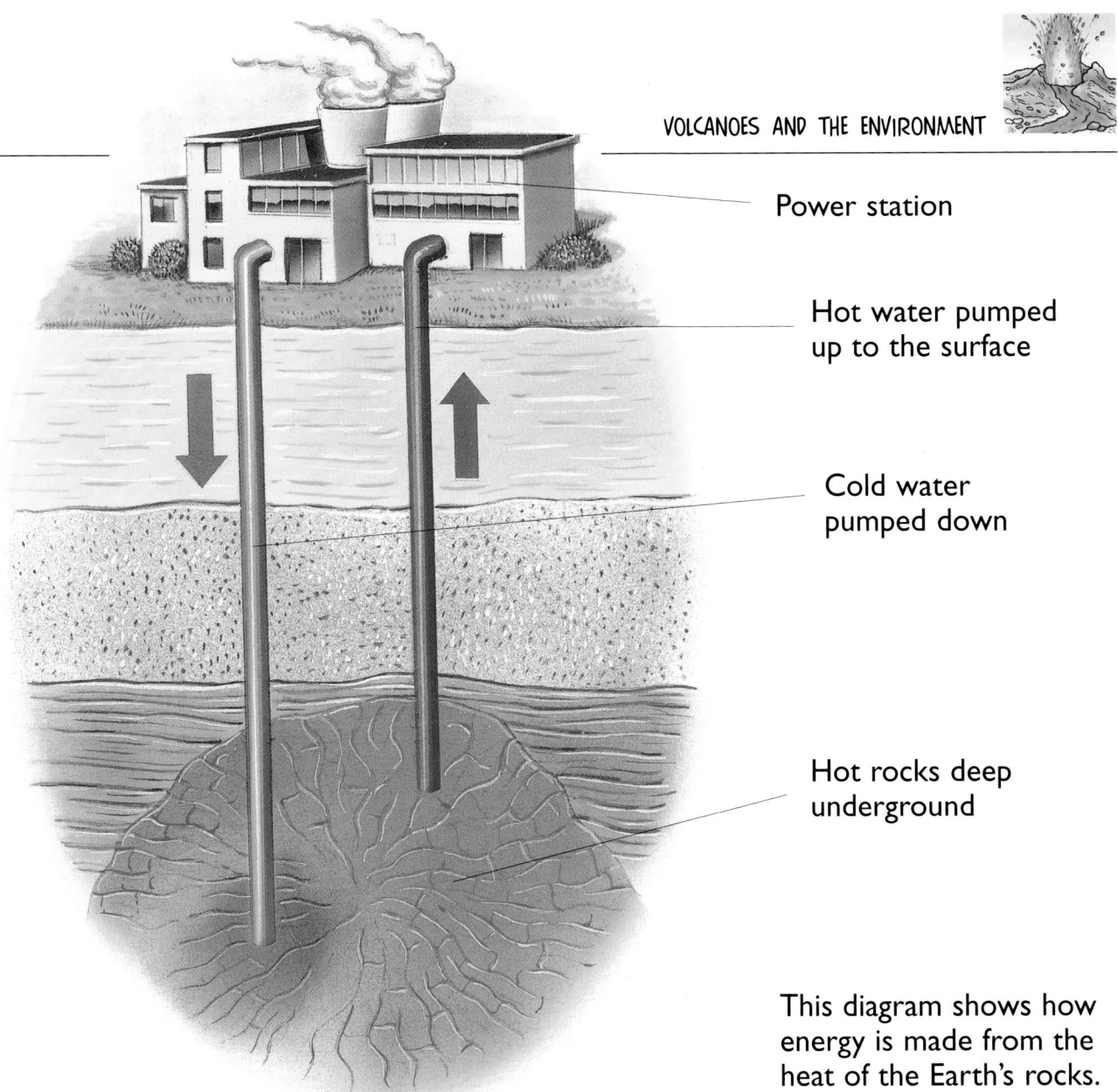

Power station

Hot water pumped up to the surface

Cold water pumped down

Hot rocks deep underground

This diagram shows how energy is made from the heat of the Earth's rocks.

Heat from volcanoes is called geothermal energy. It can be used to make electricity. Cold water is pumped down to the hot rocks deep under the Earth's surface. The rocks heat up the water and turn it to steam. The steam is then piped to a power station on the surface.

PREDICTING VOLCANOES

Scientists can sometimes work out when a volcano is going to erupt. Special equipment can show them where magma is rising to the surface. The gases coming from a volcano also give clues to what is happening underground.

This scientist is going to study the crater of Erebus in Antarctica.

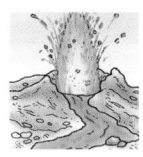

When a volcano does erupt, scientists usually know where lava, mud flows and ash flows are likely to go. But there is not much that can be done to stop them. If people live near a volcano, they have to be ready to leave quickly when it erupts.

Sometimes people try to stop lava damaging towns and farmland by building a wall of earth and rock in its path.

VOLCANO FACTS AND FIGURES

The world's loudest eruption

When Krakatoa (in Indonesia) erupted in 1883, the massive explosion was heard on the island of Rodrigues, which is 4,776 kilometres away.

The worst volcanic killers

The most deadly eruption in history was Tambora, Indonesia, in 1815. It is thought that 92,000 people were killed by huge ash falls and by starvation. Many people starved because the ash falls buried the fields and destroyed all the crops.

About 36,000 people died following the eruption of Krakatoa in 1883.

In 1902, the whole town of St Pierre, on the Caribbean island of Martinique, was destroyed by an ash flow. Only one person survived from a population of 28,000.

When Nevado del Ruiz, in Colombia, South America, erupted in 1985 it set off massive mud flows. The mud flows gushed down the mountain at 90 kilometres per hour and buried the town of Armero. About 22,000 people died.

The longest lava flows

The longest ever known was the Roza flow in North America, which happened about 15 million years ago. It stretched for 300 kilometres and covered an area of over 40,000 square kilometres.

The longest since records began was a flow from Laki, in Iceland, which was about 70 kilometres long.

The most active volcano

Kilauea in Hawaii, USA, has been erupting continuously since 1983.

The tallest geyser

The tallest active geyser is Steamboat Geyser in Yellowstone National Park, USA. It shoots water and steam up to a height of 115 metres above the ground.

The Waimangu Geyser in New Zealand used to reach a height of more than 460 metres, but it has not erupted since 1904.

Further Reading

The Violent Earth CD-ROM by Sally Morgan (Wayland, 1995)

Volcanoes, Closer Look At series, by Jen Green (Watts, 1996)

Volcano, Eyewitness Guide, by Susanna van Rose (Dorling Kindersley, 1992)

Volcano, Violent Earth series, by John Dudman (Wayland, 1992)

Volcano, Earthquake and Hurricane, Quest! series, by Nick Arnold (Wayland, 1996)

Volcanoes and Earthquakes, Restless Earth series, by Terry Jennings (Belitha Press, 1998)

Mountains and Volcanoes, Young Discoverers series, by Barbara Taylor (Kingfisher, 1995)

Volcanoes, Worldwise series, by Penny Clarke (Watts, 1997)

Hills and Mountains, Geography Starts Here! series, by Brenda Williams (Wayland, 1997)

GLOSSARY

Ash Small pieces of magma, less than 2 millimetres across, which are thrown out from a volcano.

Ash fall Small pieces of magma that are blasted out of a volcano and then fall back to Earth.

Ash flow Particles of volcanic ash from an eruption, which are blown down the sides of a volcano by hot gases.

Crater The bowl-shaped mouth of a volcano. Craters are caused by eruptions.

Crust The Earth's surface layer.

Dormant Asleep. A word describing a volcano that has not erupted for many years.

Eruption When magma, gases and ash are forced out of a weak spot in the Earth's surface.

Extinct Dead. A word describing a volcano that has not erupted for thousands of years.

Geyser A spring that shoots jets of hot water and steam into the air.

Lava Liquid magma that erupts from a volcano and flows over the Earth's surface. Lava eventually cools to become solid rock.

Magma Hot, melted rock that is found beneath the Earth's surface.

Mantle The layer of rock beneath the Earth's crust.

Minerals The natural substances from which the Earth's rocks are made.

Mud flow A mixture of hot, volcanic ash and water which flows down the side of a volcano.

Pressure When something is pressing against something else.

Devil's Tower in Wyoming, USA, is all that remains of an ancient volcano.

INDEX